Whispers Between The Pages

By Paige Celeste

ISBN: 979-8-218-79201-5

Published by Heart of the Paige
Cover Design by Paige Celeste

Printed in the United States of America
First Edition

To the quiet strength behind me
and the loving push ahead of me,
thank you for holding space for the version of me
who needed this book to be written.

This book is part of that becoming.

In the silence of ink and paper, hearts speak what the mouth dares not to even whisper.

– Paige Celeste

Table of Contents

Overthinker   6

The Weight of my Own Breath   9

Beauty in Brown   13

Nobody Has Me   15

The Kind of Woman I Pray to Be   17

The Rock and the Rope   19

The Shelf You Put Me On   22

Tying My Shoes At The Starting Line   26

Before I Begin   28

Blurry Sights   31

Embrace the Soft   33

The Sea Within Me   37

The Quiet Heartache   39

The Measure of Enough   43

No "For" In My Beauty   47

Whispers Through the Rain   49

A Soul At Rest   52

Where Love Lives   54

My Angel   57

A Seat At My Own Table   60

The Friend Who Fades   63

It Was Never Your Fault   66

A Heart I'd Hold   69

Echoes In Broken Words   72

Where (My) Worth is Known   75

The Space You Left   78

Overthinker

I try to keep up with reality versus fiction.
But sometimes,
I get so caught up in my thoughts that I can't tell the
difference between the two definitions.

My mind is a sea of things,
With all kinds of stuff living within me.
Sharks with teeth,
beautiful corals,
Barbies and brats,
Instagram and TikTok,
God,
Love,
Books,
Deeper things in darker little nooks.

Did he ever even care?
Why didn't I get an A?
Am I good enough?
Did I try enough?
Am I making excuses for something I shouldn't?
Maybe I'm being too mean… or too nice.
I have to set boundaries.
Maybe they didn't mean to hurt my feelings and
leave me in the depth of night.

I wish my mind were as calming as the morning breeze,
quiet before the day begins to weigh down on me.

Unfortunately, my mind is only quiet when I'm zoning out
from the reality of things;
when my eyes aren't focused and my body is stiff with tension.
Peace isn't much of a thing for someone whose mind runs in
circles,
keeping my body in a constant state of delirium.

One hundred miles a minute, one hundred things to think of,
to second guess.
What am I doing with my life?
Is this something I really want to commit to;
or is this just something I should use to decompress?
Somehow, even that's too slow for the things I want to do for
myself.
It's like I can never move fast enough for what I'm thinking about
in my head.
It's better for me to write it down as it comes and try to make sense
of it.
But my pen can't move at the speed of light.
Writing down what my thoughts are only goes so far.
My hand is aching and I can't write with all the emotions that I'm
feeling.

Lord, help me express and understand all the things my mind is
causing my heart to start feeling.
Did you mean it the way I read it?
Or did I read it in a different tone than what was intended?
The questions overpower me,
Causing anxiety to force its way through me.
Paralyzing me from the inside,
tearing me apart piece by piece, second by second.

Do you like me how I like you?
Are you angry?
Am I annoying?
Questions, questions with no answers to follow them.
A lot of the time I don't even ask with the fear that
maybe my ask will be the last straw for everyone around me.
That my need for reassurance will be the downfall to
everyone in my life who cares for me.

◆

The Weight of my Own Breath

I have days where I feel like I'm drowning.
My anxiety is at an all time high.
The world is on fire,
people are dying.
Humanity has become less concerned about having empathy and
more about comparing unhappy endings.

I look on social media as a way to feel better,
but it's like everytime I scroll it's another disaster unfolding.
They're saying it's the end of the world,
but they've been saying that for years.
Nobody knows the day and time,
but I'm struggling with constant fear.
Consistently in a state of fight or flight,
my mind is always on some kind of negative insight.

I'm trying to grow closer to God,
but that's such a hard concept for me to grasp.
What do I do when prayer feels like I'm crazy just talking to
myself and hoping... someone hears me at last.
I know what I feel when I listen to worship music and I have so
many role models in that "industry"...
yet it's not enough.
I don't know what to do and my life constantly feels... tough.

I want to be healthier,
but that requires money.
I want to be more productive,
but my energy is constantly flying away.
I want to be kind,

but I always feel annoyed.
I want to enjoy life,
but it feels like a constant pain inducing chore.
I don't want to just not be here anymore,
but I don't want to really do... anything I adore?

What do you do when your mind is the cage you're trapped in.?
What happens when the very thing that makes you sad is the very
thing... you can't rid yourself of?
I'm trapped in my own head,
screaming and pleading to get some sort of relief and to feel
happy for longer than a brief period for a certain thing.

It could be worse,
and for a lot of people it is.
I feel bad for the way I feel because I have no reason to feel like
my life is too much to live.
It's more of a mental and emotional thing,
I'm so hard on myself that mentally I haven't accomplished
anything.
I know I shouldn't neglect my own feelings simply because others
feel worse.
I can't help but feel for others but also— for myself,
so my body is always drained and my heart feels heavy and I need
help.
I don't have money to do anything.
I pay my bills and leave.
I can't afford to do any extra things.
It's draining to look at my account and think what the fuck is
happening?

I have the degree, I spent the time,

Why is that not enough and I always want to sit up here and cry?
I want to be healthier but my mental health is depleting.
God is my savior but sometimes I feel like I'm a really hard person
to start saving.
I have a constant sense of doom,
or sadness, or anger.
I just want to be happy and enjoy who I am without the constant
wonder.
Wondering if i'm good enough,
wondering what my career should be…
Am I a writer?
An entrepreneur? A musician? A content creator?
What am I supposed to do?
How am I supposed to live?
How do I go through the same day over and over and be happy
when I feel like I have nothing left to give.
I want to post content,
but the idea of being seen cripples me.
All of that attention on me and my life is terrifying.
But it's what I genuinely like to do.

I love to record and take pictures,
I want to plant and grow in tune with mother nature.
I want to cook more and enjoy different foods.
I want to move out and go to my own tune.
I want to write my poems and publish them too.
I want to read my books and escape to a different set of rules.
I want to open my business and see it flourish soon.
I want to travel and see different cultures and history too.

But everything feels unattainable,

like no matter what I do I won't be successful.
There is so much happening in such a short span of time.
When did I sign up for the newsletter to all the
bad news and crimes?
When did I sign the lease for this shitty season I'm in?
When will it be my time again?

I feel like I'm floating in the sea
and the waves are getting a little high.
My head is almost underwater
and I'm trying to just not panic and sink to the bottom....
and no longer be able to see the sky.

✦

Beauty in Brown

The eyes are the key to the soul.
Your eyes are like the soil,
Giving life to the trees and stability to roots spreading within your
minds unseen.
Taking one look is like a breath of fresh air… to all the plants of
your life and people you hold together when they're in despair.
Home to all the emotions that you buried deep within..
Like seeds waiting to sprout when it rains and thunders outside
again.
Holding the key to all the little things that make you the beauty we
have the grace to be able to see.
Without the soil, the flowers wouldn't bloom,
The bees wouldn't pollinate,
And the trees wouldn't be home to so many tiny tunes.
Your brown hues are the **foundation** of the most beautiful of
gardens… which is you.

The brown skin you possess holds history and an ancestry nobody
can take away.
The skin of your mother, your father, your grandmother, or maybe
a mixture of all…
A tapestry woven with profound grace from hands that didn't
withhold from the tenderness of a lover's hold in private space.

Your brown is a staple on this earth, rich as the sun's intense gaze.
A hue that carries the world's delight and amaze.
Smooth like honey that the bees freshly made,
Your brown turns into shades of mahogany,
Soft to the world's hard mockeries.
Brown eyes that appear to melt into golden rays.

It speaks to the earth in the most discreet
and innocent ways.

With those brown eyes, or skin, or a combination of both...
comes a beginning and an end.
Your brown eyes, brown hair, and brown skin will be the thing
people notice and remember the most when you're not here.
Your features that you may see as plain are what set you apart in
someone's mundane.

Your skin holds the wisdom your ancestors carried,
Your eyes tell a story of blessings and hardships you've had to
keep buried.
Your gentle brown hands are from the centuries of women who
worked for them to be that way.
Your brown is a timeless piece... that's unique to you and your
family tree.

Cinnamon and ginger, rich and deep.
So full of dimension, like a poem alive and breathing...
Standing on its own two feet.
From your eyes, to your freckles, and every curve you possess... a
history is written and you are preserved in the words and memories
of someone else.

So, they may not be blue,
Or green,
Or any other color you may think you desire;
But the gold you possess feels like a warm, comforting fire.

✦

Nobody Has Me

I wish I could say I'm not a lonely being.
How does one enjoy their alone time but constantly feel a pit of
loneliness sinking into their belly.
I can barely breath, my eyes are watery, but nobody's here for me
to talk about my despair.
It's just me.
That's all I have.
Myself with my pens and paper writing as fast as I can, typing
away to make poetry and write words that have meaning and can
be displayed.
I don't get a single call or text on my day to day.
If I don't do it nobody seems to move a muscle,
I'm the variable in everybody's lives that can always be put in a
bag and trashed.
The person whose presence doesn't hold weight.
I have friends but I'm always the one who has to sit and wait.
I beg and I plead, begging for you not to leave only for you to do it
anyway.
So why bother?
Was being gentle and vulnerable a mistake?
Maybe I shouldn't have even attempted to give more of myself
again,
   only to be disappointed in the heaviness of your absence.
It's not that I don't have anybody,
It's that nobody genuinely has me.
I'm the person who's always there,
But who is always there when it comes to mc?
Is that a controversy?
A hot take I shouldn't say?
I'm just writing my feelings down on this page;

Don't take it as hate or shade.
I love you and I hope you love me too.
It's ok to leave. Don't stay on my behalf, I've grown used to people walking away.
I'm ok in the silence of being alone in a room with no one else to entertain.
My own mind is my safe haven and my writing is my saving grace.
I'll be okay.
Even if your energy doesn't work in companionship with my space,
Just know I'll always be here and love you at the end of the day.

✦

The Kind of Woman I Pray to Be

I want to be the woman that people call
  when they need someone to pray for them.
  A woman who is beautiful within her heart,
  and outwardly in grace.
  A woman rooted in a promise
  that only God can give her.
  A woman with kindness and joy
  as the seed that grows within her heart
  and takes over her entire being.

A wife who supports and comforts her husband
  in times of need.
  Who listens before speaking,
  who offers peace, patience, and understanding.
  A wife who gives sound advice,
  and provides a safe space within her home.

A mother who cherishes and teaches
  with love and gentleness.
  Who celebrates her child no matter
  what path they choose to walk.
  A mother who mirrors the softness of God's love
  through every touch, every word, every moment.

I aim to be the kind of woman
  remembered for her heart—
  not her looks,
  not for the clothes she wore
  or the way she styled her hair—
  but for the warmth she gave,

the truth she stood on,
and the peace she left behind in every room.

Let my words be honey to the soul—
gentle enough to comfort,
strong enough to convict.
Let me lead with grace,
love with intention,
and forgive as I've been forgiven.

I want to walk closely with God—
so closely that when people encounter me,
they feel a little closer to Him, too.

Let my legacy be the light I carried,
the love I extended,
the faith I clung to—
even when it trembled.

Because I don't just want to be a woman…
I want to be *His* woman.
Set apart, spirit-filled,
anchored in a love that will never fail.

✦

The Rock and the Rope

Sometimes I just want to stop texting
and see who remembers I exist.
That's how much of a ghost to the world I feel I am to the
people I care so much for
yet there's never any persistence.

If I don't reach out, who will?
If I don't plan the day,
I'll never see you again.
I guess it's time I stop the delusion
and see what's true and real:
that sometimes,
people see you as replaceable…
not something they need
in their life to feel stable
in a world that already feels unreal.

I can't keep hoping that you'll remember me.
Consideration is the key
to the door of relationships.
Romantically and platonically,
you never consider me.

A tug of war
with someone who's barely even playing.
You've tied the rope around a rock,
and I just keep pulling.
I'm exerting myself over and over again,
tiring myself out
while you scroll on your phone
and send reels to people you actually care about.

It's okay.
Loneliness is something I've grown close to.
I'm used to being alone,
seeing everyone has their person
while I only wish I could have
the kinds of people they do.

Comparison is the thief of joy;
this I'm aware of.
But it's hard not to compare
when you see everywhere you're lacking
and you're someone everyone seems unaware of.

My poetry is my outlet,
the words I cannot say but constantly think.
I read books to feel love and support
those kinds of things.
I can make a world
with only my thoughts and the tips of my fingers.
I write them on the page
for those who feel alone in this world.

I see you.
I hear you.
It's hard to be the one who's always alone.
Even though I enjoy my space,
I just wish I had someone.
Someone to talk to,
to hang out with,
to feel connected to
on a deeper level than surface...

But that's just not something I think is for me.

I'm meant to be the support,
the backbone to other people and their feelings.
Everyone can fall against me
or turn on me...
but what happens
when I begin to do that same thing?

✦

The Shelf You Put Me On

I feel like the biggest idiot there is for caring about you.
All I ever get is hurt by you,
yet I can't seem to loosen the grip you have on me.

You promised to stay,
but you did the opposite.
You said you cared,
but honestly, it feels like you don't give a damn about me.

I feel abandoned,
left to collect dust while you place me on a shelf.

Again and again,
I give you the benefit of the doubt.
I am patient,
and loyal,
and understanding of your situation…
but damn.
Can you even see how bad you're hurting me,
thinking you're doing the *"right thing"*?

Maybe it's the right thing for you,
but for me,
it's killing me.

I sit and I cry,
begging to understand why.

Why would God allow me to fall for a man who feels he isn't
ready to give me the love I crave for me?

Why would God let me be yet another girl
who got her hopes up
for something that only ever happens when I'm dreaming?

I feel stupid.
I feel crazy for wanting to wait for you
because you don't deserve that...

But my love isn't measured
by how much you're deserving.

You say you don't want to give me a half-hearted love,
but this—
this feels half-hearted
in literally every sense of that word.

It feels like you want to keep me on a string,
giving me just enough for me to stay
and not get over you...
but not enough
to fully commit
and give me what I'm expecting of you.

I love you.
I love you even when you don't love me.
I love you even though you don't deserve
to hear those words come from me.

You hurt me over and over again.

I get so excited
only for you to shoot me down again.
You shoot me down

just to tend to my wounds
and do it again.
It's a constant, tortuous cycle.

When is enough… enough?
When will the time be right?

You don't want to force something when the time isn't right,
but honestly—
it's sounding like
you don't want to be with me and I promise that's alright.

You just want to keep me from the one
who will show he wants me.
I don't want to believe you're a liar
and all of this is a facade.

Why do I have to be on the sideline
for you to feel comfortable enough to evolve?
Why do you want to keep me at a distance,
offering me fake promises and things you know you won't do
at all?

Every time you say,
"I'll call you back,"
and you never do.
Or,
"When I get off work, I'll call,"
It's like a repeated broken tune.
Something you say
that you will never commit and do.

Almost like how you say,
"I'll stay…"
but you never do.

✦

Tying My Shoes At The Starting Line

I'm in a constant state of limbo.
I have wants,
but no desire to make them a reality.

It's hard to dream such big things,
but feel paralyzed in the state of being you don't want to be.

Nothing in my life feels certain.
I'm in a space where things change and life just gets harder by
the day.

I have to keep moving and hope it gets better
at some point in time,
in some way.

Where do I start with trying to get my life together?
I can do so many things,
but it's too much to think;
What am I doing wrong?

I scroll past lives
that seem to be already running towards finish lines,
while I'm still setting up
and tying my shoes.

It's always *"just start,"*
but I never know where to start
or what to do.

I'm constantly trying to inspire myself
with empty affirmations
and quiet prayers.

All I truly want is a map
that tells me exactly where.
Or to see the face of God
and know exactly what's expected of me
in the midst of this wear and tear.

I know I'm not alone,
and I know I'm so young.

But this is a thick fog
and knowing those facts don't always clear the haze.

My mind is loud,
my feet are heavy.
Every day blends into a daze...
filled with kind ofs and maybes.

Getting there isn't a straight line.
My progress is slow and unseen to me.

But I just have to keep breathing,
keep hoping.
Maybe my change will happen
where I at least try to get up and stop with the moping.

✦

Before I Begin

I prefer to live in the shadows—
a name with no face,
a sound with no distinct direction.

Sometimes though,
it's nice to be seen.
For my hard work to be acknowledged...
but then again,
why would I desire such attention?

Why would I work so hard
to perfect what I love,
just for it to be picked apart?

It's nice to live in the unknown of the world,
away from all the faces
and unprovoked opinions.

But what does it mean to be invisible?
What are the costs of those desires?
To be untouched by praise,
but also unseen when in pain?

To give the world the softest pieces of me
only for them to float in the abyss of nothing,
unnoticed and unnamed.

I'm safer here.
Within me.
Behind the curtains,

where it's quiet
and I can dream.

My worth isn't up for debate,
my dreams can't be dissected
and misinterpreted
by those who never dared to dream themselves.

Still—
there's a pumping beneath my ribs,
a voice that whispers in my mind:

Maybe they'll understand this with time.
Maybe someone will see me as me;
not as a target for their buried cruelty,
but a truth
clothed in tender feelings.

But I cannot help but flinch at the thought.
Some won't see art,
they'll see incompetence
in an area where I am so smart.

They'll see weakness
and they'll begin to aim their darts
at everything I'm still working to defend.

Then I'll have to gather what's left
and try to mend.

So I whisper my truth to the quiet wind,
behind a screen
where I'm the only editor—

and the only reader
that needs to comprehend anything.

I don't seek applause.
Maybe one day I'll have the courage to begin.

If my words, my artistry
find one soul who dares to transcend,
then maybe it's worth what I can't defend.

But for now,
it's not for the masses;
maybe it's just for friends,
who will hear my heart
and not just pretend.

✦

Blurry Sights

How much clearer can her love be shown?
She has said it in every way she knows;
speaking endlessly,
yet somehow
you never seemed to hear her.

What more can she do?
She's chasing after you,
being the glue that holds
the things of her and you.

She's just praying
it doesn't all fall apart.
She wants you so badly,
but you're not even willing
to run the race toward her heart.

And still,
it's only you.
Other men pass her by,
yet she watches *you.*

It's sad, honestly,
to see a girl who gives so much
to a man who isn't willing to simply do for her too.

How she sits there and bares her soul
while you just starc into space,
So focused on a single star you don't recognise the galaxy
trying to catch your eye.

She was an open book.
He was illiterate.

She read from her own pages,
straight to him.
He didn't care to listen to the words she spoke,
to get a sense of her true energy,
to see that she looked at him like he was everything.

Even when to the outside,
he should have been considered *nothing*.

You don't care to hear from her…
let alone actually pursue her.
But still she cares
more than you think.

I see you.
And in you,
I can see everything
that you ever dreamed of happening to you.

Remember that you are everything.
Even when others can't see
the way your heart bleeds
and the way you're begging to be perceived.

✦

Embrace the Soft

It is not a curse to be sensitive.
To feel what other people overlook.
To see the sadness in someone's eyes
when they don't get what they want.
To notice how the body tenses
when a certain topic is brought up.

Being able to feel
can get overwhelming,
but it's people like you
that keeps the world spinning.

You keep compassion in the spaces
where judgement is always heard.
You have patience in a so non-patient,
 always-in-a-hurry world.

People's pain doesn't amuse you.
Hatred doesn't run through you.

This is a blessing that so many people
will try to take from you.

So explore the world
in the X-ray lenses gifted to you.
See what others miss and take so lightly.
Showcase that feeling your emotions can be so freeing.

Love freely.
Cry daily, if you need to.

It's okay to be sensitive
and know that as a part of your character…
because so many people
don't have this trait that you fortunately do.

They're mean;
and expect laughter that they often get.
But if the roles were reversed, it would be a different
demeanor.
They push and shove,
trying to act tough,
but in reality,
they're insecure and drowning
in their own mind and stuff.

You feel everything so deeply,
intensely,
and completely.

To have a sensation
that touches your soul is a gift.

So act like it.
Stand boldly in it.

Feel more.
Comfort more.
Love more.
Persevere more.
Create more.

Never let someone blow out the fire within your heart.
 Don't let the clouds cover your stars.

So much empathy and kindness would be lost without you.

You are needed in spaces where it's completely dark.

Because sometimes all we need as people
is to be heard,
to be understood,
to be cared for in some way…
and you do that so effortlessly in every way.

Let them call you soft,
as if softness is not the thing
that nurtures life itself.As if rivers don't carve valleys
with their gentle persistence.
And flowers don't bloom
within the softness of wet soil.

Let them call you a cry baby,
as if crying doesn't release
an immense amount of tension.
As if it doesn't take strength to open
and stay that way regardless of the weight of heavy pessimistic
visions.

To love despite the hurtful words
and things being thrown your way.
As if feeling,
despite the aches and pains,
doesn't take more than what they do
pushing everything down and out
throughout their day.
As if holding space for others isn't something
we've been built to do from our very first conceptual day.

You—
You are quiet yet revolutionary.

Fire to ice.
The heat that melts slowly
through the thickness.
The weight that falls gently
 and erodes at a pace
 not very quickly.

Your feelings are not a flaw.
They are what make us human.
The way we were intended to be from our initial days.

◆

The Sea Within Me

Isolation and avoidance…
when my love language is quality time.

I want to experience life in its purest form…
and in divine time.

Unfortunately for me,
looking in the eyes of others
feels like I'm diving into a sea of nothing.
Complete darkness encapsulating me,
making it feel like I can't breathe.

I speak in silence.
My love is words of affirmation,
but I seek nothing.
Too afraid I'll be embarrassing,
the laughing stock of this entire thing.

Why do I fear looking foolish?
Why does it drain me to think I do?
Why can't I be carefree?

It's like a constant weight is dawning on me,
lingering like clouds,
like ships lost and drifting at sea.
I'm surrounded…
and all I can do is float.
The urge to panic rises,
but it won't do anything for me.

It's unfortunate,
but it's just me.

I've come to learn to live with the thousands of voices in my
mind
comparing,
questioning,
crowding.

It's a normalcy I believe,
to feel one thing
but know the opposite of that feeling.
To sit with that tension and call it peace.

I must learn to be okay with my own place,
my own pace—
of success,
of learning,
of becoming more than I thought I ever could be.

I get so stuck in my mind,
I force what I don't want
and push away
What I truly do,
what I truly can be.

I don't know maybe one day,
my heart and mind
will move together—
a seamless transition
of thoughts and beautiful endeavors.

✦

The Quiet Heartache

What does it mean when your actions don't match what your
words are saying?

It means telling me it's sunny outside
when I can clearly see the rain.
It means telling me I'll get roses
when all I have received is stems and thorns,
cutting away.

It means telling me you know me,
but can't even name my little pleasures on a day to day.
It means giving me just enough to keep me here,
but depriving me of the things
I truly want and need to feel okay and near.

Near to your heart,
Near to your mind,
Near to the person you hide behind a disguise.

I want romance and dates.
I want the flowers and the little notes
to show you're thinking of me in your day.
I want to feel your love and see it too.

No text back,
no dates being planned.
Why am I even wasting my time
being with this kind of man?

I see the good,
and I'd hate to say you're bad,

but man, you're making it hard
for me to feel anything but sad.

I don't want a nonchalant man that ignores me,
until he feels like my presence is worthy.
A man who makes me cry
and then sits there
and acts like he doesn't know why.

Why would I sit here
and allow myself to hurt
with this miserable guy?

I want to be worthy of your time,
all the time.
I shouldn't have to change who I am
to fit into your space.

I want you to miss me
when you wake up for a new day,
not just when the sky is dark
and now your boredom is hitting you in the face.

And not just miss kissing me
or things that require physical intimacy.
I want you to miss holding my hand,
making me laugh,
and putting a smile on my face.
Texting my phone to hear about my day,
or simply giving me a call
because I'm only ever a call away.

But you don't do that anymore.
Instead, I've been crying
and begging God to show me
the colors of your heart and more.

I just want honesty and consideration
from the man I hold close to my heart
and adore.

I feel crazy sending you a text
just to get no response.
I care about you so much,
but I genuinely wish I didn't at all.

It may seem dramatic to say,
but my chest hurts when you don't bother
to check in throughout the day.
I'm not saying we have to text every second,
but at least send me good morning at the start of your day...
or check in on me when the earth is pouring heavy rain.

I just wanted simple things from you.
I wanted what I gave to you.
I don't require much
and a lot of times I won't ask.

Why do you feel like you can give me nothing
and I'll still be yours to have?
I don't deserve to receive nothing at all,
I think at least you could give me the phone call.

My heart yearns for yours,
while I believe to you
I'm just a pretty girl you wanna feel like is yours.

Yours to hold,
yours to kiss,
your trophy locked away in a case.
Your woman that only you can embrace,
but the embrace is only in a public space.

I want more than surface,
but that's all you're willing to give.

How many times can I say the same thing
before it's me begging you,
Which is something I'm not willing to do.

What does it mean when actions and words don't align?

It means having to leave you,
no matter how bad it hurts me.
It means having to put me first,
and maybe one day…
you'll add instead of taking away from me.

✦

The Measure of Enough

What does it mean to fail?
I've always had a negative connotation about the word
'failing.'

As a child,
academic validation was something I craved—
to feel like my boat was still sailing.

Without excelling,
life felt bleak...
like I wasn't good enough
to even sit down and speak.

I know they meant well,
when they instilled the need to be good...
but what happens when good isn't enough?
What happens when my best isn't enough for you
or the world,
for society to deem me worthy of a life undisturbed?

I know they meant well
since it did me some good.
I've graduated with a high GPA,
Top 15 of my class,
a degree in business
a year earlier than I should have.

I am good.
I didn't fail... right?

But again,
what does it mean to fail?
What does it mean to be successful?

Is my best enough to be the success my parents can brag about?
To move into the adult life I sought out,
to be the role model my little sister can think about?
Is it enough?

Like being lukewarm,
I spit out the things I'm not the best at.
I don't want to fail,
so I need to succeed.
But how does one succeed
without failing at some things?

I can't help but notice
that I am bad when I desire to excel.
I feel lazy when I just want my dreams to propel.

The lukewarm is spit out in the presence of God—
you're either all in or all out,
but sometimes that's so hard.

I'm hard on myself
because it's all I've been able to do.
I can't control anything else
other than how well I do.

Disappointment is the one emotion
that I never want my family to feel.
I live for them
and try to cater to their appeal.

But what about mine?
What about my own personal need to heal?
I want to do better,
but sometimes it feels like
the enemy of doubt is strangling me.
I'd try so hard
and still somehow...
This could've been better coming from me.

My eyes wander farther and farther,
things getting harder to see.
The list of things
I'm just good at is unbearably long,
and I hate to even see that kind of thing.
I don't bother to try
to compete or communicate what makes me feel weak.

Perfection is the goal
I'm constantly trying to seek.
I can't just be good,
to me, that's too bad.
Perfection is the thing
I can't ever seem to grasp.

It's a disease of my soul—
hurting and making it hard to breathe,
tattooed across my mind in permanent ink.
I doubt myself...
and what it is that I'm capable of.

I write,
I erase.
I create,

I efface.
What is good enough for me?

Tormenting me like a ghost in this machine,
I feel like someone constantly must humble me—
question my worth,
make my art seem to be much worse.
So the question, again,
must arise:

What does success mean?
What is enough *for me*?

◆

No "For" In My Beauty

"You're really pretty,"
in the *pretty for a black girl* kind of way.
Why do women of color have to be pretty
in a certain pretty way.
I just want to be beautiful because beauty is me.
Why do you look at my dark skin
and think I cannot be.

Let me be pretty and just that.
Pretty is not a comparison,
not a word weighed down by the limits of one's perception.
It is whole. It is enough by itself.
A lot like the people you tear down
because of the skin they wear in confidence
and don't place it on a shelf.

Don't dress my beauty in conditions.
Don't fold it into small boxes
and present it to me in disguise of your hatred filled ambitions.
My beauty doesn't need a disclaimer.
It doesn't need to be said that
my skin color is darker.
My blackness is okay
and shouldn't be a deciding factor;
that my hair has more curls,
that my nose has a hump of structure.
My pretty does not shrink
to make space for your comfort.

We are carved from deep-rooted strength;
the echoes of our ancestors run deep within.

Each curl, curve, and shadowed hue
is a story of survival and love reigning through and through.
Her beauty is not an exception,
not something to be measured
against a standard that never considered us
in their societal successions.
My skin is onyx, obsidian,
the universe's canvas at midnight.
My features do not need softening,
do not need taming,
do not need shrinking.

I am not pretty *"for a black girl"*.
I am not an insult wrapped in a compliment,
not a jewel only able to be seen
when the light hits it.
I am just pretty.
Black girls are just pretty.
We are breathtaking without the need of a "but".
We have a beauty that does not ask to be named.

So take back your sentence,
the small box you tried to place us in,
your backhanded phrase.
There is no *"for"* needed when describing my beauty,
there's no need to explain.

I am.
We are;
and that is enough.

✦

Whispers Through the Rain

I feel sad today.
I feel like my world is coming down,
heavy rain being spit out from the clouds
that once gave me shade…
A break from the sun's intense rays.

I woke up today, and the motivation was:
"It's going to be okay."
Will it be?
Will I have some good news today?
Will the blues residing in my heart go away?
How can I be so sure of what, when, or if it will be okay?

"It's going to be okay."
Going signifies possible future tense.
Maybe not now, or in the near future—
but eventually, the clouds will lighten
and the wind will cease.
The sun will poke out,
playing peek-a-boo with the ground,
giving light to all beautiful things.

I prayed.
I took communion, remembering the body
and the blood that was spilled for me and you.
All of God's children have been redeemed and renewed.
I listened to a self-help audiobook,
finding peace just hearing a way
to change my mind's everyday tune.
Then I switched to worship after a few chapters.
I needed to listen to something

that speaks to my heart and soul too.
Anything to get my mind off
that antagonizing worry
that's making me feel consumed.

I cried myself to sleep the night before,
and today it seems my eyes aren't yet too sore
to cry more than I did before.

I can barely get the song out
as I'm driving along.
I want to try to at least hum the tune,
but my throat is tight.
My vision is blurred,
I'm fighting back tears,
trying to gain control over my own sight.
My heart feels heavy, my body is weak.
All I want to do is lay down and sleep,
or even just sit and never speak.

My friend got me a Bible;
a simple pleasure I embrace.
Another version of the Word
I try to live by on a day-to-day.
I ordered a coffee and a croissant
to make the day feel a little new.
One more simple pleasure
to help bring the light
and stay off the darkness of night.

"Have a great day! :)"
I've never gotten a note on my coffee cup before so why
today?

Thinking everything over,
I feel like God is comforting me in His own way.
I may not see Him,
but I get the chance to witness Him in every play.

Thank You, Lord, for listening
and being with me in Your perfect way,
comforting me to keep going
through this heavy day.

> *"Peace I leave with you; my peace I give you.*
> *I do not give to you as the world gives.*
> *Do not let your hearts be troubled and do not be*
> *afraid."*
> — John 14:27

✦

A Soul At Rest

I have an old soul,
I crave quiet and peace.
Not the parties or noise,
or the chaos that won't cease.
I wish my soul weren't so wise and so grown,
that I could live young, carefree, on my own.

I long to lose time,
to laugh without care,
with friends by my side staying up all night,
with no worry or fear.
But I want something more sincere...
That's not my way; I'm just not drawn here.

I don't have the friends who share in my grace,
those who find beauty in the stillness of space.
I've grown so used to the quiet and calm,
the silence feels like a soothing balm.
I'm so used to my own presence,
I don't even notice people's absence now.

I escape in a book, in a world far away,
or paint on a canvas where my colors can be on display
without the unnecessary eyes and chatter with so much to say.
My fingers on keys as I write with delight,
A story untouched by the world's harsh insights.
Fingers dancing on keys, weaving songs of my soul,
where every note breathes life and makes my heart feel a little
more whole.

I find joy in the simple, in moments so small,
a flower that rises, the earth's quiet call.
I can sit and think for hours on end,
in my peaceful retreat, where thoughts drift like clouds,
and time has no need to bend.
I don't need the noise, the loud, frantic sound
of people who're lost, spinning round and round.
Chasing the high, just to quiet the mind,
but the peace I seek is the rarest to find.

Sometimes I wish I could just let it go,
and share in the laughter, the life full of glow.
But my old soul finds its comfort in still,
in nature's soft hum, and the world's quiet will.
Where silence speaks louder than any sound,
and peace is the rhythm that echoes around.

✦

Where Love Lives

I love too hard…
and sometimes too quickly for my own good.
I'm so eager to showcase my love
it almost feels like I'm overcompensating
so they'll want to stay with me for good.

Some may say I should treat others how they treat me,
but why would I want to hurt someone else
simply because they have hurt me?
I refuse to let the world drain me of the love I want to receive.
I treat others how I want to be.

I want to be considered,
to be seen,
to be heard even when I'm not talking about anything.
How can I refrain from giving when I also want to receive?

I see life through a lens of pink and red,
Some people are more pleasing
because that's how I make them in my head.
The danger seems far away, a tiny speck in the distance,
but sometimes the risk is closer
then it seems through the lenses.

I can't help the love I feel overflowing inside my mind,
no matter the pain they've caused me
I'd never want hatred to make me blind.
I want to love who I love fully
without the thoughts of when…
or if…
it'll come to a teary eyed.

To be loved is to be seen.
To be seen means understanding things
even when they aren't sewn with perfect seams.
Sometimes the seams are jagged
and there may be a hole in the fabric of the sleeve.
It's okay to be a seamstress
for tiny fixes on certain things.
A needle and thread,
to listen and comprehend,
to hear one another.
That can create a beautiful, unique, patterned blend.

I want a love so pure and so intimate,
where the lines aren't blurred
and I'm wondering if they'll ever commit.
When I think of love,
I think of the things that can only be seen
between the covers and in dreams.

It's not the covers of the bed
that hold you and me,
but the pages that keep you coming back
just to experience the magic in between.
Perfectly pressed pages,
smooth black words,
and gently placed seams.
Smooth, like a river flowing
gently between the mountains' peaks.
A moment of silence,
away from the views of the world.
Love is patient and love is accepting.

I want the best for you…
even if to you, I mean nothing.

✦

My Angel

From the one who misses you.

I think if God created one close to perfect person, it'd be you.
Like pottery, you were crafted to perfection for this world,
for my family,
for our life.
Placed on this earth as a soft, yet colorful girl.
Like a painter, God mixed watercolors to get a pretty blend,
He built our family in shades that would perfectly mend.
Your laughter was yellow,
Your hair was brown,
Red lips as a staple—
every photo of you had a smile.

But now you're gone,
you're not here for me to call.
I can't hear your voice in a voicemail you'd leave me.
I'm stuck with Facebook memories
and keeping the videos of you in my back pocket,
a broken record and I don't ever have the strength to stop it.

It left us all grey.
We're slightly dimmer in color when it comes to your day.
We remember you with heavy hearts,
but we celebrate your life as a family parade.
Every year turned a little duller
as we remember your shine that faded away.

God called you home,
and selfishly I wish we never got that call.
I still remember the night,

being told to stay strong
even though all I wanted was to break down and cry.

My angel is my inspiration,
in life and in death.
I hope you can feel the love we still hold for you.
"Love never fails" is the Bible verse you adored
and we placed it permanently on our skin
as a reminder of what we need to center.

Like honey, you were sweet.
Easy on the mind and gentle to the soul,
 our love ran deep.
I remember staying up playing card games
well into the night until it was time
to go to sleep and say goodnight.

Your absence is different.
It's weird and unfit,
often, it feels unfair—
but I like to think heaven couldn't wait
to get you as an angel so quick.

Even now, your legacy lives on.
We celebrate your life every year,
and it never gets easier, even as time passes on.

Your laugh was infectious
and something I'll never leave behind.
She was like a warm blanket on a rainy day,
A comfort show that you always go back to press play.

Like Winnie the Pooh said,
"Sometimes the smallest things take up the most room in your heart."
My heart is full at the thought
now that you've finished your stay and must depart.

✦

A Seat At My Own Table

No more bare minimum,
I want the moon and the stars.
If I'm an author I want a reader,
someone who sees and digests even the silent parts of me,
using context clues to understand
the depths of who my character is written out and shown to be.

If I can write an entire book,
why would I settle for half a page of love,
just okay, just enough.
I keep picking the guy like I'm only picking for me.
But this is a man who may be my husband,
what kind of dad would he be?

He's cute. He's tall.
He seems to be a genuine soul.
But are his actions consistently genuine,
or does that sometimes fall?
Is he generous?
Does he listen to comprehend,
or simply hear just to speak?
Does he want to be a husband—or a dad?
Is that a dream in his heart,
or are you just a body he wants to see?
A title he doesn't want to be,
but also doesn't want you to be free.

It's not enough for him to want a girlfriend,
a wife,
a vessel meant for breeding.

He needs to want to be a partner,
to be a parent.
He's cute in the way that
leaves you crying by the end of the week.
He's gentle in a way that only exists in how he speaks.
But when it comes to emotional intelligence…
oh, that's nowhere to be seen.
Isn't it strange how mentioning something that bothers you,
so valid, so normal in hindsight,
turns into another fight?
I'm only in my twenties… I can give grace.
Sometimes I think I may be more mature for my age.

He wouldn't even look up to my face to fully see me,
yet I'm catering to them
like a good American woman should always be.
I'm holding a plate I can't eat,
a bottle of water I can't drink,
hoping he'll finally see me—
but instead, he's taking my seat.

I deserve more.
I give myself more than he could ever give me…
So why am I settling for things far beneath me?
My friends treat me more like a queen than he,
offering their time before I even have to ask.
So no.

No more bare minimum.
I'm the author of my own book of life,
and I can write whatever I desire to see.

No more place-fillers.
I don't want a boyfriend to take up the space
where my husband should be.

✦

The Friend Who Fades

When I'm alone on a saturday night,
no calls, no messages—
not a single notification in sight.
I wonder why.

Why am I never the friend who gets the invite?
Never the one they call just to get some insight.
I'm always there, yet never seen,
a figure lost in the chaos of its surroundings,
a shadowy figure in a world of clear pictures.
A background character to all their unfolding stories.

I don't blame my friends—
it's not like I like doing what they're doing.
I don't like the clubs,
the parties,
crowded rooms anxiously needing to feel full.

But I do wish they'd remember me
when it comes to making the quieter plans,
the kind where silence feels like company,
where the music doesn't need to have the room shaking.

I reach out,
I plan,
but plans fade,
excuses stack,
availability unravels.

And so I stop.
I will stop trying.

I wonder if they notice my absence.
If I went ghost,
would they feel the space I once filled?
Would they notice a thing?

Some may say those aren't friends,
but they are.
 I just said "no" too many times to their plans.
And eventually they stopped asking.
They said "no" to the plans I'd try to sew together,
ripping the seams—
and, unfortunately,
I don't feel like stitching the pieces that keep separating.

◆

!! Content Warning !!

This poem contains references to sexual assault and victim-blaming. Please take care while reading.

It Was Never Your Fault

You were born into a world filled with lustful eyes.
The craving for 'just sex' is a little too normalized.
From childhood your dad told you *no guys...*
He didn't trust their intentions when they met your eyes.
"They only want one thing"—a saying said *so* many times.

Beautiful to all the guys,
a pleasure to their eyes.
But when it comes to hearing your mind, those eyes just... die.

Pretty face, nice hair, clothes too tight—
or too loose, depending on the weather outside.
Perfect teeth, expressive brown eyes, or blue or green,
or maybe they look a little dead inside.
Slender hands, long legs, or short legs with thicker thighs.
My shirt is too big, no wait, too small.
She's showing a lot of skin or maybe she's showing none at all.

Sexualized and romanticized without the need to try.
Blamed for others' actions
when you didn't even realize the thoughts
that were running wild in their minds.
They hide their intentions behind a "nice guy",
 or maybe they don't,
and the predator is right in sight.

It's not your fault they decided you were less,
simply because you're a girl in a dress—
Or maybe in shorts, baggy jeans, sweats,
a baggy t-shirt, a vest.

A cardigan with a skirt,
tennis shoes and my hair a mess,
no makeup, or with makeup.

I was at a party with my "friends,"
or maybe in my home with the comfort of a boyfriend.
It was my family, and my family would never hurt me.
She was just a little girl and
they said it was okay and a secret between the two parties.

He was my husband,
so that can't be true for my experience.
But you didn't like it—or maybe you did, at first.
But you said no or stop,
or felt confused or felt lost.
It's okay to take consent back whenever you want it to end.

Does anyone care now?
It's been years since it happened.

Maybe if he wasn't so known?
Maybe if he wasn't considered a "nice boy"
they'd believe what was shown.
"He sleeps around with everyone, what did you expect?"
"He's your boyfriend, he's going to want sex!"
"Well you kept flirting with him, I see why he made a move."
But your discomfort should be enough
for everything to stop and never continue.

You didn't expect to be violated
and your "no" to be considered a "yes."
If I don't give them attention, I am ugly and rude.

I risk him taking rejection negatively
and resulting in harming me.

If I do give them attention,
I run the risk of them becoming obsessed with me.
Not taking my no for an answer
or letting me let them down gently.
When something happens, it's my fault all over again.
"What were you wearing?"
Does it really matter?
My clothes shouldn't have anything to do with this subject
matter.

You know…
it's not your fault.
It never was,
And it never will be.

You deserve to be treated with the utmost decency;
whether you show off your body
or dress more discreetly.

You are a woman,
and it's not your fault
where their minds choose to be.

✦

A Heart I'd Hold

I want a gentleman.
Not just when we're out in public,
but even in private.
Someone who holds the door open as I walk into the restaurant,
pulls my seat out for me,
sits right across from me.
Someone who's okay just holding my hand.

I want a considerate man.
Someone who doesn't make me cry when I answer the phone,
who doesn't say "*I'm on the way*" when he never plans to
come at all,
someone who thinks of me when he makes simple decisions.
Because when I like someone, they become my centerpiece;
the thing that brings the whole room to life, even in its
simplicity.
I want you to pick up the phone and show me you care.

I want a soft-spoken man.
A man who doesn't yell or set a negative tone,
but speaks with love
and reassures me when I'm feeling a little in the unknown.
A man with gentleness in his voice,
a calming aura that's pleasing to hear;
someone who doesn't immediately shift me into a defensive
gear.

For me, I cater to a man who treats me well.
Show me you love me,
and I'll show you a million times as well.

I want a gentle man.
A spirit filled with love and tenderness.
One who cries in moments of weakness,
finds peace in my arms,
and doesn't care about the idea of being emotionless.
A man who is kind, yet assertive.

I want a genuine man.
Truthful and honest in what he feels for me.
I don't need someone who lets me believe in a fantasy.
Express who you are, authentically.
Don't manipulate me into thinking
you're already the man you're only dreaming to be.
Let me accept you for who you are, openly.
Build a foundation of trust and connection with me.

I want an attentive man.
One who notices the little things—
the small changes within me.
The man who remembers the outfit I wore on our anniversary,
picks my favorite flowers right from the ground for me,
listens to me ramble about what bothers me
or what I simply find pretty.

Honestly, just be genuinely interested in me.
Write me the little notes I need to hear
so my mind stays clear.
Prove to me daily that I'm not just someone passing through;
that my feelings matter
without the need to condemn or compare them to you.
Take responsibility for hurting me,
Even if that wasn't what you intended to do.

Call me before bed.
Take note of the boundaries I place.
I want a man who makes me feel safe.

Safe to be feminine,
Safe to submit.
I don't want to wonder if you'll ever commit.
I shouldn't have to text you a million times just to get a reply,
or be afraid to speak my heart
because you'll turn it into something we can't even try.

I want a caring man.
One who wants to know me inside and out,
who listens when my soul speaks through my mouth.
A man who never wants to be the reason for my tears.
Who'd tear the world apart just to help me conquer my fears.

I want a man who sees me,
who notices me,
 who considers me in his thoughts and actions
 even when I'm not in the room to express my satisfaction.

◆

Echoes In Broken Words

The words you speak are the world I know.
My wind is your voice, soft and free,
or harsh and damaging.
The trees are me, moving in your gentle breeze,
or being knocked over in the midst of your insanity.

You live in my head,
the voice that keeps on talking, going and going,
sometimes in circles, just to keep me from exploring.

You feel the need to own me,
telling me sweet words,
but then it's like a switch is flipped
and suddenly it sounds more like a curse.

Do you love me or do you hate me?
By your actions, I'll never know.
Your words say you love me,
but the way you look at me
gives me so much anxiety though.

My head is spinning, and my world is unclear,
uncomfortable with the ghost of your love
playing like a ring in my ear.
Annoying and loud,
your words used to put me at ease
and make things clear.
Now I'm stuck in a cycle I can't seem to break,
whether you're far or near.

Your words are a bandaid
on the wound you decided to make.
I'm trapped in a way where you control me.
You speak, and I move—
like a puppet,
my arms and hands tied to strings,
forcing me to stay on tune.
I don't have a choice...
or at least it feels that way for me.

How can you say you love me,
then turn around and make me bruise and bleed?
You swept me off my feet... quite literally.

My hands in yours,
in a tight embrace,
my body moves to a beat
I can't even begin to make.
Honestly, it feels like all you know how to do is take.

I follow your tune
and hope it makes you happy enough
to show me that your love is true.
I try to set the tone.
I try to make things work with you,
but you only seem to move
at a pace that's fit for you.

I fell victim to your words...
slow dancing in a room of mindless bliss.
Yet your truth lies behind the eyes,
behind the way you treat me with so much despise.

Your eyes show me the truth
that your words so easily disguised.

For a moment, though, I believe you.
Your words give me the desire to remain,
to stay in your arms like a jacket when it's cold.
I remain in the hurt,
which is the embarrassment
every time I allow you closer and fold.

I yearn for your words... of affirmation,
but I also yearn for them to be true.
Did I ever stand a chance against your wordy kiss?
So vulnerable like a child,
but I'm not naive enough to realize
that delusion isn't bliss.

Your words were meant to trap me
and leave me broken and bleeding,
but luckily your actions
were the things that helped me in my fleeting.

I can see that the words you speak,
and the words I hear,
are only the version of you
that I want to appear.

✦

Where (My) Worth is Known

It sucks when I'm not shocked anymore.
You can leave today,
and it'll look like you never left out my front door.
I'll continue to go
and pretend you never existed at all,
because you always leave.

You leave when things aren't a comfortable call.
If it gets too tough,
you decide to let go and just forget it all.

I won't fall with you.
I'd rather do this on my own with a broken heart
than settle and be unhappy with you
in a place that I never sought.

I can't force you to want to do it for me,
let alone with me.
If you wanna leave, you'll leave…
like you always do.

Oh, sorry I brought up a conversation you didn't wanna do.
I guess I'll just have to walk on eggshells
and pray my feet don't get cut up and bruised.

Oh look… there's another time you weren't there.
I didn't expect you to be anyway, to be fair.

Yet another time you couldn't look me in the eye
and say something that was fully true.
You decided a kinda sorta lie would suffice.

It's all you seem to be able to do
because you live in a disguise.

A disguise of this "good guy,"
when in reality,
you couldn't show me a good guy in your life
that you didn't let pass you by.

So stay stuck and in your ways.
Don't talk to me and try to make some plays.
The answer is no.
I'm done with this.

As much as I want you,
I know that I can get more than this.

There's a man who will want to do it for me.
Who will want to hear me
 so that we can fix things.

A man who is courteous
and considerate of my heart.
Who holds it with gentle hands
to ensure it doesn't feel pain whilst in their care.

The lack that you give
is one he'd never fathom.
He'd at least try to make me happy
in the ways I can imagine.

My someone isn't someone I'll have to force
to spend quality time with me.

He'll do it simply
because he wants to see me.

If you don't have time,
it's okay.
You don't have to make time for me.
Just let it be.

So I'll say it again.
It sucks to not be shocked by your lack anymore.
But you can talk like a broken record,
make your promises,
and forget them as you go.

I will be finding my partner
who is, and gives,
much, much more.

◆

The Space You Left

I hate when sadness sneaks up on me.
When I start to think about you
and everything I'd love to build
only for reality to slap me awake once again.

I miss you.
I miss the kind words and hand holding.
I miss feeling wanted and heard when I'm upset.
I miss feeling seen when I'm stressed,
not as a girl with an attitude that always causes distress.

I miss your voice,
the way it carried comfort even from a distance.
I miss your face,
the way your presence softened the edges of my day.

It was never just the physical,
it was the things I couldn't hold,
yet felt the most.

Anyway,
tonight I'm thinking about you,
about the conversations we'd have.

It's crazy how misunderstanding,
inconsideration,
and absence
can strip away so much of what we had.

✦

To the One Still Reading

If you've made it all the way here, thank you so much for giving me the opportunity to speak with you through my poetry.

Thank you for sitting with my words, for letting them echo, settle, and maybe even stir up some things within you. Every poem in this book came from a place I stood, and still may stand to this day. I wrote these in the midst of feeling the loneliness, heartache, confidence, and everything in between. This book was a cry out, a release of deep emotion from my own heart, barefoot in emotion, arms open to truth. Some pages were hard to write. Some I cried all the way through. Others, I breathed through with ease. But all were open and honest, true to what I was feeling at the moment.

I hope somewhere between the pauses and punctuation, you felt less alone. That a piece of your story was swimming in these pages for you to find. Because this book is not just about me, it's about those feelings that we all feel but may not have the courage to say in the light of day.
It's an invitation for you to feel seen and be seen too. You are not alone in this, I promise.
If anything I've written gave you a push to heal, explore, love, and live unapologetically then I've done all that I needed to do.

Carry these whispers with you. Let them live in your journals, your prayers, your silences. Let them remind you that your voice matters, what you feel is valid and real, and who you are becoming (regardless of the bad) is beautiful.

About the Author

Paige Celeste is a poet, storyteller, and lover of quiet moments where words and emotions intertwine. A graduate of Sam Houston State University with a degree in Business Administration, Paige's journey into writing has always been fueled by a deep desire to express the raw, tender spaces of the human heart—unpacking loneliness, hope, faith, and the complex beauty of becoming.

Her love for writing began as a young girl, finding comfort and clarity in putting her thoughts to paper. Over time, her poetry grew into a sacred practice of vulnerability and healing, creating a sanctuary not only for herself but for readers to find their own reflections between her lines.

Paige is the voice behind the podcast *Heart of the Paige*, where she shares deeper stories and readings of her poetry, inviting listeners into a space of reflection and connection.

Whispers Between the Pages is her debut poetry collection, born from the whispers of her soul and offered with love to anyone seeking to be seen, heard, and understood.

Acknowledgments

This book is a testament to the power of persevering through the sadness and anxiety of being vulnerable and taking the chance to just go through life in honest expression. I would not have brought *Whispers Between the Pages* to life without the incredible people that I've shared moments and conversations with along the way.

First, to God, who is my constant source of grace and guidance and unfailing love. Even when I drift far from Him and my path feels unclear, my thoughts are weighing heavy on me, the love and light I receive through those times is a work of mercy indeed. You've planted so much within me and I'm finally pushing through the anxieties to grow those seeds.

To my family, thank you for your unwavering support, even when you didn't always understand where I was going on this journey of finding my place. Your love has been my safe haven, the place I know I can always return to when the noise of the world is becoming too loud and overwhelming.

To the one who has loved me so gently and pushed me to do whatever I want, thank you for seeing me, for listening to my words and speaking life into me. Thank you for telling me I can do anything and for holding space for both my strength and my softness. Your quiet presence has been a balm to my spirit that sometimes feels hot and scorned with doubts and anxieties. Your belief in me gave me the courage to press 'publish' on my heart.

Thank you to the readers, listeners, and growing community for picking up this book and spending your hard earned money on it. Knowing that my words resonate with you reminds me that I'm not alone, even when I am my most silent.

Finally, to every soul who has ever felt lost, unseen, or unheard... this book is for you. May it give gentle caresses for your heart and remind you that your feelings are valid, your standards are valid, and your voice and journey matters.

With love,
Paige C.

Let's Stay Connected

Just because we've reached the final page doesn't mean our time together has to end!
If you found pieces of yourself within these whispers, I'd love for you to join me beyond these pages.

Heart of the Paige Podcast: Found on Spotify, Apple Podcasts, & YouTube
Step behind the poems with me! On my podcast, I speak softly regarding my poetry to share reflections, behind-the-scenes meanings, and reading select pieces from this collection aloud. It's girl talk, soul talk, and truth unfiltered. You're already invited and it's open and free for any of you to enjoy!

Connect with Paige:
Follow along on my personal social media for more poetry, creative musings, and glimpses into my daily life:
Instagram: [@paiigeclst] For poetry snippets, creative inspiration, and everyday musings.
TikTok: [@paiigeclst] Short-form reflections, behind-the-scenes of my writing process, and playful content.
YouTube: [Paige Celeste] Vlogs of my life, creative projects, and everyday moments.

I'd love for you to join me in these spaces! Let's keep sharing, growing, and creating together!

www.ingramcontent.com/pod-product-compliance
Lightning Source LLC
LaVergne TN
LVHW051706080426
835511LV00017B/2765